Will our children be

HOW WILL OUR CHILDREN GROW?

Christy Kenneally

VERITAS

First published 1998 by
Veritas Publications
7/8 Lower Abbey Street
Dublin 1

ISBN 1 85390 364 7

Design: Bill Bolger
Cover illustration: Angela Hampton Family Life Pictures
© Angela Hampton
Cartoons: John Byrne
Printed in Ireland by Paceprint Ltd, Dublin

SOMETIMES MY PARENTS CAN BE A LITTLE TOO OVER PROTECTIVE..

KEEP OUT

SOMEONE HAS WRITTEN, 'Once you have a child, you must learn to live with your heart outside your body for the rest of your life'.

That's how vulnerable we parents are.

I remember sitting in the kitchen at home listening to the radio with my father. As the news listed the wars and disasters of the world, he would plough through the paper, as if he was unconcerned. But, if the story was of a drowned child, then his face would tighten with pain, and he would cross himself. I wondered at his reaction then, I don't now.

Which one of us doesn't skip certain stories in the newspaper, or turn off the telly at certain pictures? More often than not, these deal with the hurts inflicted on children and we instinctively move to protect ourselves from the possibility that such terrible things could happen to ours. We are vulnerable, so we protect our vulnerability.

Is it right to be careful? Of course it is. We live in the real world. Distance is a natural defence against worldwide calamities; faraway tragedies affect us less because they are far away. but, in the real world of instant news, nowhere is far away any longer and disasters come to all communities.

Is it right to be careful? Yes. But our carefulness can cause us to be defensive. We can easily put up barriers against such possibilities; we can keep our children in and keep them close and when we do, even then, there is no guarantee that trouble will pass us by. As hard as it is, we must face up to the fact that hurt must come to us and to those we love. What then can we do to protect them?

Sometimes, an old story can throw fresh light on a modern question. The Bible is a collection of stories. Many of them deal with people learning to live with one another and with the reality of their God in a real world. Let's take a leaf from the Book of Jeremiah.

His people had learned to live with their circumstances and the ordinary troubles that came their way during the natural cycle of their day-to-day lives. And then, a disaster threatened from the outside. Invaders were coming and a whole way of life was threatened. The usual arguments were put forward. 'We'll fight them.' Imagine, a group of small farmers taking on the might of an empire. That was a non-runner for starters. Talking of 'runners', maybe some of the people suggested doing one. But who could run faster than a chariot or a trained horseman?

Jeremiah asked God for help. Maybe he was hoping for a decent plague that would waste the invaders like the one that decimated the Assyrians, or maybe the kind of flood that had halted the Egyptians. What he got from God was silence. At first he was disappointed and disillusioned.

Then he watched the village potter at work. This man took clay and threw it on the wheel. He dug his hand into it and it rose up on either side into the shape of a jar. If it collapsed, he simply started with the same clay all over again, perhaps shaping it in some other way. If the clay was moist and supple, it could be

shaped and reshaped again and again. But, once it was fired in the kiln, it became brittle. If it was shattered then it was gone forever. Watching the work of the potter, Jeremiah began to realise something amazingly important. When we can't destroy or avoid something that troubles us, we must adapt to it. We must go out and face the new reality, take it into ourselves and make something of it. Is that what Jesus meant when he said, 'If you would be follower of mine, take up your cross daily'? That means, don't wait for it to happen you, or have it thrust upon you, go out to meet it and take it into yourself and transform it.

To get back to our children – if I create a fort around my child, the reality is that all my effort will not stop the walls crumbling before the real hurts of the world. Also, those walls I built to protect him may even become his prison, limiting the height of his growth and the length of his flight. And, when I'm gone, who will protect him then?

Someone once said, 'Rear your child to be an able orphan'. Which means, help him to cope with the real world so that, when he stands alone, he may be strong enough to live well with anything life brings his way.

'But, I'd hate to expose him to the hurts of the world.'

No parent worthy of the title would invite hurt on their child, but trouble comes, invited or not. The question is 'Will he be equipped to deal with it?'

'I'd hate her to lose her innocence.'

There is a huge difference between 'innocence' and 'ignorance'. A child who is equipped with knowledge is a child in control. How she is equipped with that knowledge is very important. Isn't there a big difference between hearing the 'facts of life' in the security and normality of your home, in the comfort and love of your parents and as something that is beautiful and God-given, and becoming acquainted with them in the mutual ignorance and fear behind the bicycle shed? In that sense, a person can live a long, real and wholesome life and still die 'an innocent' if they have been equipped with a mind and heart that is founded on what is good, loving and of God. To leave a child 'ignorant' is to leave her in the dark. And what parent, worthy of the name, would do that? The dark is a space in the mind that is open to phantoms. Remember the story Jesus told about the man who was possessed by demons? When they were thrown out, the man replaced them with nothing, and so the demons came back, even more numerous than before, and 'the last state of that man was worse than the first'. If we don't roll up the blinds of the mind and fill it with the light of 'innocent' knowledge, then it can easily become a place of distorted shadows.

Yes, of course it is important to be careful, but not care-full. It is natural to have times of anxiety but it is not healthy to become an anxious person. It is right to defend our children against the hurts of the world but the best defence is a strong and loving mind and spirit that can face, feel and transform whatever comes.

Where do we start?

You know the old story about the tourist in Kerry who was foolish enough to ask directions of a local. 'Arrah', said their guide, 'If I were you I wouldn't start from here at all.' Sometimes, our starting point is wrong. We ask ourselves, 'what can I help them become?', rather than 'who can I be for them?' I once asked a wise man to tell me how I might raise a good son. I expected him to answer 'By being a good father'.

He surprised me. 'Be a whole person', he said. I think he meant that a child who grows up with a whole person has a good chance of being whole. I'm also glad he didn't say, 'Be a good partner', because not every parent has a partner, and I'm especially glad he said 'whole' rather than 'ideal', because that would have knocked me right out of the equation.

Isn't there a great temptation to try to be perfect for the sake

How will our children grow?   5

of the children? In the first place, that's an impossible task for any man or woman. In the second place, isn't it better for a child to model herself on a real person and so be equipped for a real life? And in the third place, 'playing perfect' can be an awful strain on our sanity.

When they were very small our children thought that Dad was Superman and Mam was Miss World. Then they got to that awful stage when they looked at us as if we were from Mars. 'She's not going out in that. What age does she think she is?' Then they found out about sex and didn't talk to us for a fortnight. And now, if we're lucky, they are beginning to see us, warts and all, and to forgive what's lacking in us and value what's loving in us. But, if we're afraid of failure, we become defensive and stubborn when we make mistakes. So, when we do fail, we stonewall rather than admit and apologise. Imagine apologising to a child. How could you have any credibility or authority? Ask yourself, do you really trust someone who never admits to being wrong? Then why should our children? Furthermore, by never admitting to fault and asking for forgiveness, what message and model are we passing on?

Authority is an interesting word, isn't it? Too often it translates into, 'because I'm telling you, that's why', or, 'I'm the boss in this house'. Its root is the word 'author' and an author is someone who creates a work. Wouldn't it be wonderful to consider that in the acknowledgment of our weakness, we are helping to create a person who will not be afraid to do likewise. Thankfully, our real authority doesn't depend on our being ideal and perfect but on being real and willing to admit imperfection.

An author is also someone who gives life to something. The old saying holds true, 'No one can give what they haven't got'. Which poses the question: 'What about the quality of our own lives?'

'She gave her life for her children.'

This was a common compliment once upon a time. Think about that. It usually meant that she had beggared her own quality of life to enhance theirs. What message is being passed on here? Someone must be lessened so that someone else may have more. Not exactly a balanced outlook, is it? After all, healthy, whole people are supposed to be those whose needs are being met, and, a healthy family is one where each person's needs are being met. Of course, there are times when we sacrifice our own needs for the sake of others, but it would be a mistake to make that our life's work. Needy people have less to give and sometimes, sadly, expect to get it all back later with interest.

'I want my children to have what I never had.'

Not too much wrong with that sentiment, is there? Many of us owe a lot to parents who left school early themselves and worked hard, and made sacrifices to give us our education and opportunities. Now that people are better off and education is more readily available to all our children, there is a different slant to that aspiration.

I think we may have moved away from 'giving them the chances we never had' to 'giving them the things we never had'.

I met a man who had, as they say, 'done well for himself'. He told me of his poor background and how, by dint of hard work, he built up a very successful business and made himself wealthy. 'I made up my mind', he said, 'that my children would never have to go through that kind of deprivation. They would never want for anything. So, I gave them everything. Now I find I have children who never have to raise a finger. They have and expect the best of everything.' Then he added, 'by providing them with everything I never had, I deprived them of all the values I developed while working myself up to what I have today'.

It's a sad and a salutary story. You know the old saying, and maybe it's coming into it's own again, that we could end up with a generation who 'know the price of everything and the value of nothing'.

What are values?

The word has two roots. One means 'to be worth' and the other means 'to be strong'.

Let's put the two together. Values are the beliefs we regard as worth holding. And it is by living out those beliefs that we are strong and whole people.

Maybe this little story will shed some light on the power of values.

A mighty warship is sailing speedily through the night when the signals officer says to the Captain,' Sir, there is a ship's light approaching in our sea-lane'. 'Signal him to move to starboard', the Captain snaps. 'Move to starboard', the warship flashes. 'Move to starboard yourself', comes the reply. 'Do these people know who we are?' the Captain rages. 'Signal who we are and order them to move.' The signal flashes, 'We are the mighty warship Dreadnought, move aside'. The answer winks back, 'We are the lighthouse'.

Our values, our principles, are lighthouses. We can be guided by them or wrecked on the rocks on which they stand. These are the strongly held beliefs that add up to what we are worth and living them makes for a worthwhile life.

Cherish.

The constitution of a country is usually a statement of its values. Ours is very strong on the idea of cherishing all of our people equally. There are important words tucked into that sentence. Take the word 'cherish'. To cherish our children simply means to 'hold them dear' to us or to love them. A simple enough value surely, but not so easy to put into practice. Let's look at it from a few angles since love, as the old song says, 'is a many-splendoured thing'.

Love and other unmentionables

'How did you know your father loved you?' I asked a man who had children of his own. 'Sure, didn't he rear me', he answered, and I could see that he was putting that value into practice in the rearing of his own. 'But did he ever tell you?' I persisted. 'Arrah no,' he replied, 'that class of thing wouldn't be said in our day'.

I think we are getting better at saying it. I hear parents unselfconciously telling their children, 'I love you'. More and more adult children sign off their telephone calls to their parents or to each other with these words. Yes, I know, many people are afraid of falling into huggy-huggy talk; the kind of soppy phrases that can become mechanical and insincere.

'Have a nice day'

'Missing you already'

'Walk backwards as you're leaving so I think you're coming in.'

'That's not our culture', they'll say, and rightly so. But we are learning not to be afraid of speaking our love. Jesus, as you know, was a great storyteller. As an illiterate himself, I suppose he appreciated that a good story will travel from ear to ear and many of his stories have stood the test of time. The Prodigal Son is a great example of a good story, because it can mean different things to different people. The meaning we were all taught in school was that the forgiving father didn't wait for the boy to come home with his tail between his legs. He didn't wait for the long, shame-faced apology. He didn't say, 'I told you so', or, as one man famously and confusingly remarked to his son, 'Well you have buttered your bread, now you can lie on it'.

But, there are more sides to it than that. It's also the story of an older boy who was taken for granted; the 'good lad' who was

never acknowledged for his loyalty and industry. 'My son,' the father says, you know that all I have is yours?' And the son could have replied, 'Yes, father, I know I'll get the farm, but I never got the signs of love you showered on the young lad'. Being taken for granted is a heavy and a lonely burden.

By telling them that we love them, what are we teaching our children? We are saying that it is not something we say easily or to everyone, and therefore, that their status in our hearts is all the more important. We are saying that it is good and wholesome for people to speak their love to each other and that this speaking can build up a relationship. The funny thing is that we have no problem doing it with babies. I heard a woman say ruefully that most men step into senility if they get within three feet of a cot; as if there was a Bermuda Triangle there where men were guaranteed to lose their minds.

In that situation, words of tenderness seem to pour out of them quite naturally. And then, when the child arrives at the age when the man considers them 'grown up', the men 'grow out' of the habit of speaking their love. And the message to the child is clear; love words are baby-talk and not the thing for grown men. I think we should speak our love so often that it becomes second nature to us.

An Irish compliment

A 'first cousin' to speaking our love is giving them praise.
'I'd be afraid she'd lose the run of herself.'
'He might get notions.'
'There's no point in swelling their heads.'
How quickly we forget one of the great truths summed up so beautifully in the first language of the Constitution:

'Mol an óige agus tiocfaidh sé.'

Praise the youth and it will flower.

How often does the reverse happen? Instead of 'lifting up' we practice 'putting down'.

'Ah sure, 'tis easy for her.'

'Why wouldn't he do well with all that was spent on his schooling?'

'We all know what 'pull' can do.'

'We knew him when he didn't have a seat to his trousers.'

'Can any good come out of Nazareth?'

The legacy of that practice is a generation of Irish people who just cannot accept a compliment.

'That's lovely on you.'

'Dunnes.'

If we can't cope with success then we become fixated on failure; a people always in search of the flaw.

'I work for a doughnut' the factory worker told me. 'You do a hundred things right and hear nothing. You make one mistake and you never hear the end of it. Just like looking at a doughnut,' she added, 'he always sees the hole and never sees the cake.'

One of the great gifts Jesus had was his ability to see the best in people. Where others saw prostitute, he saw loving heart.

Where others saw tax collector, he saw lonely heart. Where others saw a leper, he saw a person wasting away for the want of a simple touch. His whole ministry was one of seeing to the heart and to the best in it, and, because he did so, the best in that person blossomed. Magdalen became the thirteenth apostle, Zacchaeus became a philanthropist, the leper rediscovered his wholeness as a person. 'Only a mother could love him,' was once a common and damning comment on many a child, and, surely, it was that mother's love that often proved the child's salvation. Seeing the best in them and marking it is often the first step to bringing the best out of them.

Did you have a teacher with that gift? If you had, then you'll have no bother remembering him or her. This gifted man or woman shone their light on your talent and, of course, it grew.

After the Inter Cert, I was choosing subjects for the Leaving Cert. Like many of my ilk, I wanted to fill up my quota of subjects with an easy one that wouldn't take up too much time or effort. Careers Guidance in our day was that you asked some fella in your class for advice. This was surely the cross-fertilisation of ignorance.

'Do Art', my classmate urged, 'sure any eejit could pass Art'. Art for me was the doodling I did in the margins of a copy to

How will our children grow?

while away boredom. I found myself sharing desks in the Art room with Picasso, Monet, Renoir and Modigliani. They were brill and I was useless. Our teacher was an extraordinary man. The first day, he set us doing a still life. He circled the room, murmuring praise to the geniuses. Then he came to me.

It was clear, even to the untrained eye, that my still life would still be moving long after the bell had sounded. As I braced myself for the 'bitter word', he murmured quietly, 'Very brave, Christy, keep at it.' To this day, I remember him with affection. He was a man with a loving eye for effort rather than perfection, and he taught me much about the art of living and loving.

All eyes and no sight

How do we see our children?
The nurse was new to the Hospital for the Elderly.
'How are things?'
'Oh, I'm very disillusioned.'
'Why? What illusion did you have?'
Her illusion was that people got nice as they got older.
They would be sweet, grateful and undemanding, and she would be Florence Nightingale, sailing among them happily with her lamp aloft. Of course, it was an illusion The reality is that people don't usually change radically as life progresses, they just become better at what they always were. So, if they were cranky at thirty, they'll be even crankier at seventy; after all, they've had forty years' practice to perfect it.

We can have illusions about our children; false dreams and standards that we fabricate as measures of their success. Because so many of these standards are unreal, they have no real chance of attaining them, so we are setting them up to fail. How many

parents send John to school in the morning and expect Einstein home for his lunch? The Gospel is savage about those who set impossible burdens for people to carry and then never lift a finger to help them. Is it fair to burden a child with what we'd like them to be rather than loving them for who they are?

Don't raise the bridge, lower the river!

There's another side to this 'seeing'. We can also be tempted to see them as less rather than as more.

'Ye'll be lucky to end up as messenger boys', a primary school teacher once informed us. We were delighted at the prospect. Messenger boys had bikes. I think he saw us as 'disadvantaged'. We were working-class kids, and in his eyes, we would never 'amount to anything'. Tragically, some of his pupils may have believed him and shrunk their dreams accordingly. Is it true that parents can feel protective and defensive when their children have dreams? Is it true that they are tempted to lower the ceiling of their children's dreams in case they don't succeed and so get hurt? That's why I started this section with the title of an old film, 'Don't raise the bridge, lower the river'. Let's rewrite it as 'Don't raise the dream, lower the child'. That kind of protection limits their vision and their growth. But, suppose they don't have the ability to reach their dream? There are many answers to that. Won't they have achieved more in the pursuit of their high hopes that they ever would have if that hope is dragged down? Won't the very height of their hope encourage them to greater effort? Won't they be older and wiser when they realise that they will never play for Ireland and so be better able to look lovingly on it, not as a failure in their lives but as something that gave them a reason to try, and train, and achieve. And what kind of

achievement will they have? Why, that of knowing that they did their best and achieved a great deal according to their abilities. And surely that's as good a definition of success as any.

The young man was so wrapped up in the private world of his Walkman that I didn't want to break the spell. But, I was curious. He looked so much like a cool, modern dude that I was surprised to hear Pavarotti leaking from the headphones.

'Are you into opera?'

'Yeah, sure. I'm just back from Italy, actually. I was having my voice trained'.

'What did you want to be?'

'An operatic tenor, just like yer man Luciano.'

'How did things turn out?'

His teacher took him aside at the end of his final year and told him gently but firmly that he would never be in that class, but that he had a very fine voice and could enjoy a very successful career as part of an operatic company.

'Were you disappointed?'

'Oh yeah, for about ten minutes. What I wanted was to sing and that's what I'm going to do, and get paid for it.'

That's the good part of the story, now read the rest.

He went home and told his Dad what the teacher had said. His father opened his newspaper and remarked:

'We don't rear second best in this family.'

Surely he's forgetting that a boy or girl who rises through dint of effort to be the best they can be, is never second best to anyone, because their true measurement is against no one else but themselves.

'Love their dreams and love them for dreaming them.'

How many great men and women have said that the greatest barrier to their success was the discouragement of others?

'What will you be when you grow up?' was a common question and the wrong question. It immediately suggested that the job defined the person. Happiness was when the children answered 'a priest, a doctor, a teacher'. Despair and anxiety resulted if they answered 'an astronaut, a television presenter, a rock-band promoter'.

The real question should have been, 'What kind of person would you like to be when you grow up?' because that question focuses on values like being loving, hospitable, honest, cheerful, etc. If we could only build the values then whatever they may actually 'do' will be imbued with those values.

Do you remember a time when certain jobs had 'dignity'? These were the 'professional' jobs and they had all the hallmarks of success. If you didn't manage to get into one of the professions then you just 'went to work' for the rest of your life. But no job gives dignity to a human being – we are supposed to have that from birth. The human being who is assured of dignity brings that dignity to any job they will ever do. Not all of our children will grow up to be Celtic Tigers. Not all of them will work, and if we continue to make the false connection between work and worth, how will they have any sense of dignity? They won't unless they get it straight and early that 'they are worth more than many sparrows, that the very hairs of their heads are numbered, that before I saw you in the womb I knew you.' They must be told that nothing they ever achieve in life could add to the love and regard we have for them. This must be the starting point, the bedrock of our relationship with our children. Anything extra is just that, extra.

When should we be doing all of this? We're busy people. We have jobs to hold down, careers to build, mortgages to carry, bills to meet. Need I go on ? Where will we get the time?

Now and then

When you were five, what did you want to be? Six! And when you reached six you discovered that ten-year olds had all the fun... and then... and then... all the way up to thirty, before going into reverse. The best time would always be 'then', some time in the future. And we looked so eagerly to that future that we lost sight of the present. The old people said we were 'wishing our lives away'. Isn't there always the danger that we work so hard to provide a future for our children that we neglect to give them a present. But we want to do the best for them. Yes, but are they getting the best of us?

I met a young man recently who worked all the hours God gave for his family, for the house he wanted them to live in and the schools they would go to and so on. His reasons were the very best, but, as he said himself, 'I have the best possible reason for the worst possible lifestyle'. He's afraid that he'll look up from the grindstone some day and they'll be gone. He would love to spend time with them, 'quality time', he calls it, but when he manages to fit it into his busy schedule and he's all ready for a deep meaningful relationship, they want to watch the telly or read a comic.

I told him about the woman and the pre-marriage course. It had all happened years before but she had it crystal clear in her memory.

'We were in this lovely building, out in the country, and, after one of the lectures, the organiser gave us pen and paper and told us to go off to our rooms and write down the kind of relationship we would like to have with our future children. Well, when I think now of what I wrote then! I said I wanted to create special times of quiet during the busy day, when the children and I would relate deeply with one another.'

'And how did it work out?' I asked innocently.

'I have five of them and 'tis a madhouse. You haul them out of bed in the morning in a daze, pull the pyjamas off them, pull clothes on them, swipe them with a face-cloth, bucket porridge into them, hurry, hurry, hurry and they're gone. Home for lunch, drink your milk, chew your food, don't talk with your mouth full, hurry, hurry, gone. In the evening, the whole process is reversed. Do your homework, I know no Irish, ask your father, your books are where you left them, if I have to go up that stairs again, someone will suffer. 'Laughing heartily, she added the best line of all, 'I'd say my gang were reared in the meantime.'

There's nothing mean about the meantime. It's that precious time when we're not concentrating on being good parents and are relaxed with our children. It's that time when we get absorbed in a game or in telling a story about our own childhood and find, to our surprise, that they're fascinated to discover that we were children once upon a time and weren't born at the age of forty. It's that time when the adult lets the mask slip and allows the child in themselves out to play, and at times like that we are as near to real and natural as we can get.

The meantime can be noisy or quiet, it can even include that 'damned' television, when they curl up beside us on the couch and stretch their feet for contact and comfort. It is that blessed, blessed time when we are just 'there'. At times like these, bonds are formed and memories are made.

I look back on such times with my own Dad. There were times when he would forget the factory, or the ESB bill, or the loose slate on the roof and be content just to be a presence among us, radiating warmth and security. The wheel turns. I set up a fishing trip a few years ago with my eldest lad who was all of six at the time. We would have a day on the river, I would teach him to cast and, naturally, we would catch fish and cook them on the fire. Straight out of Disney. As it happened, he wouldn't stop talking so there wasn't a fish inside the 'three-mile limit' for the whole afternoon. He cast unerringly into trees and caught his 'good' jumper on the hook, and I was demented as my perfect day collapsed around me. Just then, a kingfisher arrowed up the river and hovered before us. I was transfixed at the beauty of the little bird. 'Stephen', I breathed, and the bird vanished. 'What is it?' 'Ah, you missed it,' I said, describing the marvellous creature as we waded home, fish-less, through the meadow grass. Months later, we were lazing around at home, and, as usual, he was away in a book.

'What does enchanted mean, Dad?'

'Oh, it means to be under a spell. You know, like when a witch casts a spell on someone in a story and they are in her power'.

'Does it mean something else?'

'Yes, it can mean that something wonderful happens and, for a moment, we're full of the magic of it.'

'You were enchanted the day you saw the kingfisher, Dad.'

He was right, I was enchanted. And, in my own joy, I managed to touch him in the deepest area of his heart.

It's hard to be joyful all the time, but, we could all manage it a bit more often. There is much in the world to fear and much hidden in the future we could be anxious about, but, the fact is that all my worrying, all my plans, all my efforts cannot guarantee an extra day in the life of my child. So, I can do nothing about the length of his life but I do have the chance to do something about the depth of it. And that life and that time is now.

'There is no time like the present.'

'And no present like the time.'

What about faith, what about religion, what about God?

As the preacher said when he was twenty minutes into his sermon; 'And now, my dear people, a word about God!'.

If you're thinking that I've waited for the last minute to drag God in by 'the hair of his head', then, think again. Surely everything we've talked about up to now is about God and his relationship with us and how we are trying to reveal that God to our children.

Anyway, about God. Will our children believe in God as we do? Who can say? A man once said to his son, 'When I was your age...!' and the son interrupted gently to say, 'Dad, you were never my age!' We stand on the earth and wonder at the stars; our children will stand on the stars and wonder at worlds we never dreamed. The fantasy of our childhood is the fact of their present. Our privilege is to equip them to see the revelation of God in their own time. Surely, the God who could be revealed in a burning bush to one generation can also make himself known on the Internet to another.

We cannot educate the minds of our children and then complain if they ask questions for which we have no easy answers. Why should we fear? Why should we worry if they will find God? It is God who finds us in the womb and loves us eternally as a mother loves her child.

If we could learn to love their search; to love their unknowing, their doubt, even their rejection of what we believe or the way we worship, if we believe that each generation stands on the shoulders of those who went before, then let us clasp their ankles and support them as they see beyond what we can see. Let there be no talk of 'casting out', of 'never darken my door' etc. Remember well the woman who did not share her son's vision, and yet, never stood in his light; the woman who must have been bewildered by his choices, his friends, his words and ways, and yet who was there in his darkest hour, a fixed point of love in the chaos of his crucifixion.

Will they pray?

Yes, but probably not as we were taught to do. They will pray in their own way as they wonder at the world, as they experience the exhilaration of love, and, perhaps, at the miracle of their own children.

There are so many uncertainties before them, and, in the face of so much uncertainty, it is important for parents to be true believers. I feel we must believe in a God who is faithful and true

WHEN I WAS A KID
WE SPENT ALL OF SUNDAY
PRAYING...

YES, BUT THE
DAYS WERE
SHORTER
DURING THE
ICE
AGE!!

in his love for us and for our children, and we must believe in our children and in the God who dwells within them.

To paraphrase the promise of the Scriptures:

'What then shall separate them from the love of Christ? Shall unemployment, addiction, rejection or separation, or all the hardships that haunt their parents' dreams, all the things that might and could happen?' 'No', Scripture promises, 'We are more than conquerors through him who loves us'. Conquerors? Yes, and more; transformers, people who can take what the world throws their way and transform it into something life-giving and love-giving. How? Because they are conscious of God's living power

within them. How can they become conscious of that? Through the love we hold for them and through the example we show them. It all comes full circle, eventually, doesn't it? It all comes back to what I believe and what actual difference it makes to who I am and how I live and what I do with what life sends me. How can children be joyful if they live with pessimists, how can they rejoice in the gifts of others if they live with begrudgers, and how can they believe in any kind of worthwhile God if they live with those who are public, card-carrying, Mass-going Catholics and who are privately the living contradiction of all the values they publicly espouse? Strong language, but the subject is too important for the camouflage of fancy words. It's a bleak question, but one we must each ask ourselves: What kind of God do I believe in and what difference has it made in my life and would I hold that life up in front of my child as something he or she would find attractive.

So, will our children be okay?

Well, are they okay now? No, not are they successful in school, with troops of friends and blessed with good looks and so on, but, are they loved for who they are right this minute? If the answer is yes, then, yes, they're a long way towards being okay.

Will our Children be Okay?

Will our Children be Okay? is a series of booklets designed to explore parents' concerns regarding their children's future. In each booklet a well-known author explores one of these concerns or questions in a way that is rooted in the context of life in Ireland as we approach the new millennium. In each case the author offers advice and reassurance and hope from his or her own experience or expertise in the area.

The second title in the *Will our Children be Okay?* series is written by Michael Paul Gallagher SJ and addresses the issues of religion and faith.

WILL OUR CHILDREN BELIEVE?
Michael Paul Gallagher SJ

Michael Paul Gallagher begins by examining the parental role in religious education and encourages parents not to be neutral in passing on the faith. He cites the current interest in spirituality and the inner self as further evidence of the search for faith and the desire for expression amongst today's youth. He addresses many of the issues relating to faith and religion today, in particular the demarcation between faith and culture. Recognising that many parents have insecurities surrounding their own faith, Fr Gallagher guides those wishing to give their children every chance to grow as Christians.

ISBN 1 85390 369 8 • £3.99

More from Michael Paul Gallagher SJ
QUESTIONS OF FAITH
Michael Paul Gallagher SJ

In this stimulating discussion of some of today's major issues, Michael Paul Gallagher SJ provides thought-provoking answers to twenty-five questions asked by young people in their quest to make sense of themselves and of God. Topics addressed include: the problem of suffering, the search for happiness and life after death.

ISBN 1 85390 234 9 • £5.95

Available from Veritas and all good book stores
VERITAS

IRL: 7-8 Lower Abbey Street, Dublin 1 • Tel (01) 878 8177 • Fax (01) 874 4913
email: sales@veritas.ie • web: www.veritas.ie
Also: Stillorgan, Cork, Ennis, Letterkenny & Sligo
UK: Lower Avenue, Leamington Spa, Warwickshire CV31 3NP
Tel (01926) 451 730 • Fax (01926) 451 733

Reflections and Prayers for Young People

THE CALM BENEATH THE STORM
Donal Neary SJ

The prayers in this book reflect the hopes, worries, desires and fears of young people. It creates a centre in the rush and uncertainty of life, and the prayers are written with honesty and simplicity. The author's sensitive and realistic perception of the attitudes and experiences of young people today enliven the prayers in **The Calm Beneath the Storm.**

ISBN 0 86217 096 0 · £2.95

LIGHTING THE SHADOWS
Donal Neary SJ

Lighting the Shadows will start you praying – from your own experience, from the world about you, from some of the words of Jesus in the gospel. Some of the prayers will lend themselves to your own personal words, and might even lead you to compose your own.

ISBN 1 85390 228 4 · £3.95

Donal Neary is Chaplain at the Mater Dei Institute of Education in Dublin and is the author of a number of popular books on spiritual themes. His experience of dealing with young people stems from several years of leading retreats and prayer-meetings for young people from all backgrounds.

Available from Veritas and all good book stores

VERITAS

IRL: 7-8 Lower Abbey Street, Dublin 1 · Tel (01) 878 8177 · Fax (01) 874 4913
email: sales@veritas.ie · web: www.veritas.ie
Also: Stillorgan, Cork, Ennis, Letterkenny & Sligo
UK: Lower Avenue, Leamington Spa, Warwickshire CV31 3NP
Tel (01926) 451 730 · Fax (01926) 451 733

welcome to www.veritas.ie

FIND OUT more about these and any other **Veritas titles**

directly on our Website.

Order over the **Internet** from ANY of our listed categories.

You can also enquire about **ANY** book of interest to you.

Why not joint in on <u>our on-line</u> discussion group.
Our **CHAT GROUP** allows you to share and air your views with others.

Even if you have nothing to say,
the **<u>chat group</u>** makes fascinating reading!!!

Contact us NOW at our website...

http://www.veritas.ie

for further information contact email: marketing@veritas.ie or phone (01) 878 817